MY TIME WITH GOD

DAILY DEVOTIONAL

ART JOURNAL

first 15

©First15 2023

Illustrations by Jennie Miller
Typesetting and design by Amanda Barnhart

No part of this publication may be reproduced, distributed, or transmitted in any form or by any means, including photocopying or electronic or mechanical method without prior written permission of the editor; except in the case of brief quotations embodied in critical reviews and certain other noncommercial uses permitted by copyright law. For permission requests, please write to us.

Unless otherwise stated, Scripture quotations marked (ICB) are taken from the International Children's Bible®. Copyright © 1986, 1988, 1999 by Thomas Nelson. Used by permission. All rights reserved.

Scripture quotations marked (NLT) are taken from the Holy Bible, New Living Translation, copyright ©1996, 2004, 2015 by Tyndale House Foundation. Used by permission of Tyndale House Publishers, Carol Stream, Illinois 60188. All rights reserved.

Scripture quotations marked (ESV) are from the ESV® Bible (The Holy Bible, English Standard Version®), copyright © 2001 by Crossway, a publishing ministry of Good News Publishers. Used by permission. All rights reserved. The ESV text may not be quoted in any publication made available to the public by a Creative Commons license. The ESV may not be translated in whole or in part into any other language.

My Time with God

DAILY DEVOTIONAL + ART JOURNAL

by Lisa Clark

Let's spend time with God!

Table of Contents

8
Letter to Parents

10
Introduction

14
Day 1:
What Is a
Devotional?

18
Day 2:
Just the
Two of Us!

22
Day 3:
What Is
Prayer?

26
Day 4:
What Is
Worship?

30
Day 5:
Closeness
with God

34
Day 6:
Why Spend
Time with God?

38
Day 7:
Loving What
God Loves

42
Day 8:
Live for
Love

46
Day 9:
Renewing
Your Mind

50 Day 10: Enjoying God

54 Day 11: Our Unchanging God

58 Day 12: Our Good Father

62 Day 13: Growing Good Fruit

66 Day 14: Making the Most of Our Time

70 Day 15: The Holy Spirit in Us

74 Day 16: God Is Our Friend

78 Day 17: Hearing God's Voice

82 Day 18: Knowing God's Truth

86 Day 19: God's Loving Discipline

90 Day 20: Becoming like Jesus

Letter to Parents

Dear Parent or Guardian,

My Time with God was written for young readers, ages six to twelve, to help encourage and equip them to establish a lifetime of learning and walking with God through daily Scripture reading and reflection. This resource is foundational, answering questions such as:

- *What is a devotional?*
- *What is prayer?*
- *Why spend time with God?*
- *What does it mean to enjoy God's presence?*

As parents, we long to provide tools for our children to learn and grow, and this twenty-day devotional + art journal will help your child develop a desire to daily spend time with God now and throughout their lifetime!

We pray you find great joy in seeing your child grow in their knowledge of God, his character, and his love for them. As they complete these next twenty days, feel free to check in with them and ask them what they're learning along the way. I am sure you will be encouraged too!

God bless you and your kiddo!
LISA CLARK AND THE FIRST15 TEAM

Hello!

Welcome to My Time with God, a twenty-day devotional + art journal written *just for you*! This might be your first devotional ever, or maybe it's your tenth. Either way, we pray you will grow in your love for God and his word each day!

Spending time with God every day through reading, praying, and practicing our faith is so important for us to draw close to him and know him more. So, every day for the next twenty days, you'll do just that.

Each day has the following elements to help you make the most of your time with God:

1 Devotional: Read a scripture for the day and a short devotional that will teach you about God, yourself, and the Bible.

2 Prayer: Spend time talking and listening to God.

3 Go: Enjoy a fun activity to help you apply the truth you've learned.

Read. Pray. Go. Repeat!

As you think about the next twenty days you will spend with God, what excites you the most?

Draw or write what makes you excited.

At the end of this devotional, our prayer is that you will be excited to keep spending time with God every day. God bless you as you read, pray, and go each day with a God who loves you so much!

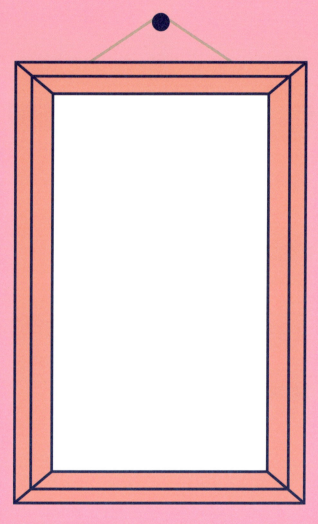

✎ **Draw** a picture of yourself with your new journal.

"Come near to God, and God will come near to you."

—James 4:8a (ICB)

Day 1: What Is a Devotional?

SCRIPTURE

We know how much God loves us, and we have put our trust in his love. God is **love, and all who live in love live in God,** and God lives in them.

—1 John 4:16 (NLT)

What *is* a devotional?

A devotional is a book, like this one, that helps us to know God more by reading his word, praying, and practicing our faith. This is *your* devotional. *Your* time with God. Every day, you will open this book, read Scripture and a devotional, spend time in prayer, and do a fun activity to help you grow closer to God.

So, let's get started! Are you ready?

Look at the scripture to the left. First John 4:16 teaches us that if we live in God, we live in love!

Circle the word LIVE every time it appears. How many times did you find it written? ☐

Another word for "live in" is *abide*. Abiding means to stay connected or to stay close to someone or something. Making time for meeting with God every day makes abiding possible.

To stay close to your parents and friends, you must spend ☐ with them! *(Hint: It's a four-letter word.)*

That's right, TIME! We stay close to those we love by spending *time* with them. We will talk a lot about that over the next twenty days as we dive into what it means to love God and others.

Let's pray together!

Thank you, God, for loving me! Please show me how to love you and others more. God, I want to stay close to you and *live* in your love. As I spend time studying your word, help me to know you better and grow in love for others.

In Jesus's name, amen.

GO   **Get organized! Let's make sure you're set up for success!**

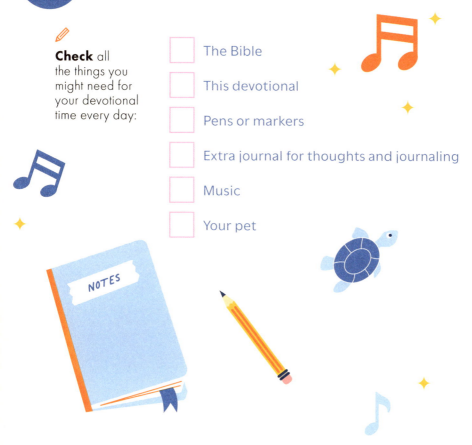

Check all the things you might need for your devotional time every day:

- The Bible
- This devotional
- Pens or markers
- Extra journal for thoughts and journaling
- Music
- Your pet

Wait else do you need? Don't forget to keep everything together in one place so you'll be ready every day for your time with God.

You completed Day 1! Woohoo! See you tomorrow.

Day 2: Just the Two of Us!

SCRIPTURE

My heart has heard you say, "Come and talk with me." And my heart responds, "Lord, I am coming."

—Psalm 27:8 (NLT)

God created us, so he knows us best. In fact, he knew us before we were even born!

Check out this verse from the Bible:

> You made my whole being. You formed me in my mother's body. I praise you because you made me in an amazing and wonderful way. What you have done is wonderful. I know this very well. You saw my bones being formed as I took shape in my mother's body. When I was put together there, you saw my body as it was formed. All the days planned for me were written in your book before I was one day old. —PSALM 139:13-16 (ICB)

God created you in your mommy's belly! How cool! He created all your body parts, your personality, and your uniqueness. He knew you before anyone else in the world knew you.

But how do we get to know *him*?

We get to know him just like we get to know our friends. Do you remember your first day of school or church? Did you walk in on the first day, pick out someone across the room, and think, "We're going to be best friends"? No! You got to know friends by playing on the playground, working on projects, and eating together.

We get to know God the same way when we spend time with him. Our time alone with God helps us know him. And, as we get to know God, we love and trust him more. Then he becomes our best friend!

Let's pray together!

God, thank you for creating me, loving me, and knowing me. I want to know you more. I pray today and every day I will spend time with you, just the two of us! Help us to become best friends.

In Jesus's name, amen.

GO Just like everything else we do that's important to us, we have to plan for our time with God. Let's do it!

What time do you wake up?

What time do you go to sleep?

What time do you go to school?

When will you begin your time with God every day?

Draw hands on the clock to show when you'll start spending time with God every day.

Isn't spending time with God fun? See you tomorrow!

Day 3: What Is Prayer?

> **SCRIPTURE**
>
> Well then, what shall I do? I will pray in the spirit, and I will also pray in words I understand. I will sing in the spirit, and I will also sing in words I understand.
>
> —1 Corinthians 14:15 (NLT)

Prayer is *talking* to God and *hearing* from God. Most of the time, we're using our words. But sometimes our spirit does the praying.

What does this mean!?

Sometimes, when we don't know the words to say, our heart does the talking. All we have to do is stay quiet and listen. It's like we're on the phone with a friend. We talk some, and they talk some. It's a conversation. That's prayer!

You might be thinking, "How do I hear from God? He doesn't talk back!" But he does. He "talks" to us through his word, the Bible, through worship songs, nature, and different people, like pastors, trusted friends, and adults, like your mom and dad.

He also talks to us in our spirit by his spirit. The closer we get to God through daily time with him, the more often we'll hear him speak to us. Do you ever have a tough time knowing who or what to pray for? Well, good news, God tells us what to do! Check out this verse from the Bible:

> Also, the Spirit helps us. We are very weak, but the Spirit helps us with our weakness. We do not know how to pray as we should. But the Spirit himself speaks to God for us, even begs God for us. The Spirit speaks to God with deep feelings that words cannot explain.
> —ROMANS 8:26 (ICB)

How cool is that? God even helps us pray!

Speaking of prayer, let's pray!

God, I am so happy that I can talk and listen to you in prayer. Please, speak for me when I do not know what to say. Help me to get closer to you through prayer every day. Thank you for loving me and being in control of all things. I love you.

In Jesus's name, amen.

GO

One more thought for today. Remember we talked about prayer being like a telephone call with a friend? Did you know God has a telephone number? He does! It's Jeremiah 33:3: *Call to me and I will answer you and will tell you great and hidden things that you have not known (ESV).*

When we have prayer time, it's easy to let our mind start wondering about other things. **Make a list** of people and things you want to pray about. You can come back to this list every day, and even add to it!

Don't forget God's telephone number. He's never too busy to talk to you. See you tomorrow!

Day 4: What Is Worship?

SCRIPTURE

Shout with joy to the Lord, all the earth! Worship the Lord with gladness. Come before him, singing with joy. Acknowledge that the Lord is God! He made us, and we are his. We are his people, the sheep of his pasture. Enter his gates with thanksgiving; go into his courts with praise. Give thanks to him and praise his name.

—Psalm 100:1–4 (NLT)

DEVOTIONAL

What is worship? How would you define it? Write your answer below:

....

....

Worship is celebrating and honoring God. We celebrate and honor simply because he is God! We can worship with our voices, our lives, our hands, and our whole self! Think of your heart having a throne in it. A throne is a place where a king or ruler sits. The throne on our heart is meant for God and God alone.

Draw a picture of a heart with a throne inside.

So, now that we know what worship is, when do we worship?

Yes, we worship at church, but we can also worship as we go throughout our whole day. We can worship in the car, at meals, during our time with God, and when we're outside in nature. When we respond with thanks and celebration to God's presence in our life, that's worship. Sometimes worship can be in the form of a song, but it doesn't have to be. It can be a thought, like, "God you are good!" or even a prayer.

Worship is thinking of God and praising him for who he is.

How do you worship God?

....

....

Let's pray **together!**

Thank you, God, for who you are. I worship you today! Draw me close to you today so that I notice you in all that I do. Help me to worship you and not just things you have given me. I love you.

In Jesus's name, amen.

GO

Let's finish our time with God by playing some worship music. While you're worshipping, see how many times you can hear the word WORSHIP. This is going to be fun! Go!

✏️ **Draw** a tally mark every time you hear the word WORSHIP in your song!

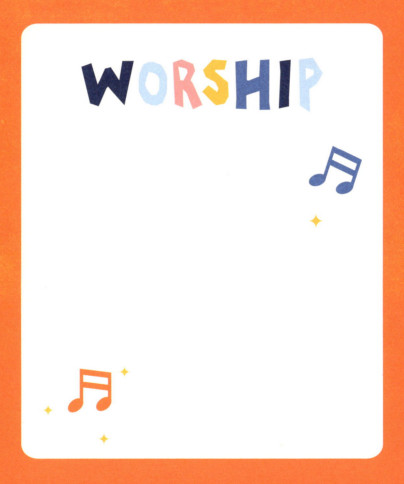

You are doing great! Keep singin'! See you tomorrow.

Day 5: Closeness with God

SCRIPTURE

Remain in me, and I will remain in you. No branch can produce fruit alone. It must remain in the vine. It is the same with you. You cannot produce fruit alone. You must remain in me. I am the vine, and you are the branches. If a person remains in me and I remain in him, then he produces much fruit. But without me he can do nothing.

—John 15:4–5 (ICB)

Jesus is the one who spoke the words in our scripture for today! He wanted his friends, and us today, to know that they needed to stick close to him. Jesus is like the trunk of a fruit tree, and we are the branches. If a branch falls from a tree, can it still produce fruit? Nope!

But if a tree is healthy, what kind of fruit will it produce? It produces the kind of fruit that grows from the trunk and into the branches. Orange trees produce oranges. Apple trees produce apples. Grape trees produce grapes. Just kidding! Grapes grow from vines in the ground.

Speaking of vines, in this passage, Jesus is telling his disciples that if they stay connected to God, they will grow good fruit.

What does that mean? It means that if we are connected to God, we will become more like him. And when we become more like him, our light starts to shine!

In Matthew 5:16, Jesus said, *"In the same way, you should be a light for other people. Live so that they will see the good things you do. Live so that they will praise your Father in heaven"* (ICB).

We need to stay close to God to know him more, and then the world will know we love him, and they'll want to love him too!

God always wants to stay close to us. But sometimes we move away when we get busy or other things crowd him out. So, in our scripture today, Jesus is reminding us to stay close like a branch on a vine. We want to stay attached so we grow to love him more and more.

Who is the vine? _____

Who is the branch? _____

Let's pray together!

Thank you, God, for staying close to me. I want to stay close to you! As I go about my day today, help me to remember you are with me. I want my life to produce the kind of fruit that shows the world that I love you!

In Jesus's name, amen.

GO **Look up Galatians 5:22–23 in your Bible.** In the fruit pictures below, list the fruit that is growing in your life. We listed one to help you get started.

Don't forget, God is always with you. See you soon!

Day 6: Why Spend Time with God?

SCRIPTURE

Come near to God, and God will come near to you.

—James 4:8a (ICB)

Congratulations! You have completed five whole days of your devotional! Isn't spending time with God awesome?

But *why* do we do it? Why spend time with him every single day?

....

....

The best part of our day is when we spend time with God, so we want to do that every day. Daily time with God connects us to him. And there are so many things we do every day that need to be done. Like brushing our teeth!

What else do you do every day?

1. _____   4. _____
2. _____   5. _____
3. _____   6. _____

When we start with the best thing, everything else seems to work out. Isn't that amazing? When we start our day with God, we go through our day with him, remembering him, and trusting him to be with us no matter what happens. When we run out of time or forget to spend time with him, we don't feel as connected to him. And that's not a good thing!

What does our verse of the day tell us? When we come near to God, what does he do?

....

Let's pray **together!**

God, thank you for this time together. I'm so thankful you want to spend time with me. I pray I want to spend time with you too! Help me remember that my time with you is valuable and important. Help me make this a priority every day.

In Jesus's name, amen.

GO

We know spending time with God is good for us. But don't forget, it's good for God too! He loves us so much and wants to be with us all the time.

 Draw pictures of ways you can spend time with God during your day.

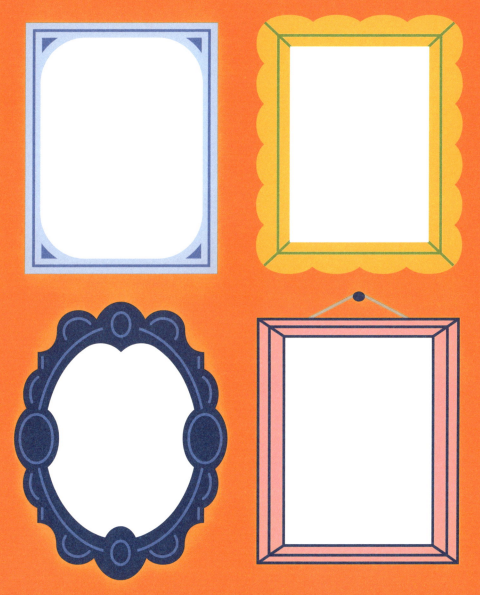

Share with your family and friends some of the ways you can spend time with God. See you tomorrow!

Day 7: Loving What God Loves

SCRIPTURE

Jesus replied, "'You must love the Lord your God with all your heart, all your soul, and all your mind.' This is the first and greatest commandment. A second is equally important: 'Love your neighbor as yourself.'"

—Matthew 22:37–39 (NLT)

We all have favorite things! Maybe a favorite toy, snack, or TV show. What are some of your favorite things?

1. _____
2. _____
3. _____

Did you know those things aren't eternal (well, unless you listed a person)? What do you think *eternal* means?

_____

_____

Eternal means it "lasts forever." Above everything else, God wants us to love things that last forever. And what things last forever? Here are two easy answers: God and people! He wants our hearts to be filled with love for him and others. If we're so focused on *things* that don't last, we can't focus on God.

Circle every time YOU, YOUR, or YOURSELF is used in the scripture on the previous page.

God wants *your* whole heart. He doesn't want you to love the things you get in this world more than you love him or his people. Sometimes we love our things so much that we put them before God. But God loves people first, and he wants us to love people more than anything we can earn or buy in this world.

People are eternal. Loving people, serving them, and sharing the love of God with them is what God wants our hearts to desire most.

Let's pray together!

Dear God, help me to love you with my whole heart! Help me to take care of the things you give me, but help me not to love my things more than I love you or the people around me. Keep my heart close to you and filled with the things you love.

In Jesus's name, amen.

GO

Put an X through the things that are not eternal and circle the things that are!

✏️ What are some ways you can show love to the eternal things in your life? Like your parents, siblings, or friends? **Draw** a picture or write an answer.

Isn't spending time with God fun? See you tomorrow!

Day 8: Live for Love

SCRIPTURE

I pray that Christ will live in your hearts because of your faith. I pray that your life will be strong in love and be built on love. And I pray that you and all God's holy people will have the power to understand the greatness of Christ's love. I pray that you can understand how wide and how long and how high and how deep that love is.

—Ephesians 3:17–18 (ICB)

We have the opportunity every day as we study God's word to know him more. There's so much to know about God, but simply put, God is *love*! His love is everlasting, eternal, higher than high and wider than wide. Oh yeah! It's deeper than deep and longer than long too.

Circle the word LOVE in the verse on the page to the left every time it appears!

Wow, that's a lot of love! ❤️

The love of God our father is everlasting. That means we can't outrun it and we can't hide from it. God's love is also unconditional. That means there is nothing we can do to make God love us less!

And did you know we can love like him? Because of God's love, we can love a friend who upset us or left us out at recess. Because of God's love, we can forgive someone who hurt us. Because of God's love, we can obey our parents with a good attitude. We have the power to do all of this because of God's love for us. And since he loves us so much, we want to honor him and keep his commandments.

When we choose to love God and let ourselves experience his love, he also teaches us how to love others. Living for love means living like Jesus did. He was always thinking of others. Here's a story that describes God's big love:

A young boy who came out of church one Sunday asked his father, "Dad, the preacher said if I ask Jesus into my life, he'll come and live in my heart. But Jesus is so big and I'm so little—won't he stick out all over me?"

That's a funny story, but it's true! If God is in us, everyone will know because he will be in everything we do. He will "stick out all over us"!

Let's pray together!

Dear God, thank you for loving me! Your love always surrounds me and never gives up on me. I'm so thankful! Help me to love others just like you love me. I pray you "stick out all over my life"!

In Jesus's name, amen.

GO

In the heart below, write as many words as you can to describe God. As a bonus, maybe put some Bible verses next to each word. For example, *loving, kind* . . .

GOD IS

Kind (Psalm 36:7)

Loving (Ephesians 3:17–18)

R-E-P-R-E-S-E-N-T! Let's represent God's love today in all we do! See you tomorrow!

Day 9: Renewing Your Mind

SCRIPTURE

And now, dear brothers and sisters, one final thing. Fix your thoughts on what is true, and honorable, and right, and pure, and lovely, and admirable. Think about things that are excellent and worthy of praise.

—Philippians 4:8 (NLT)

Our minds are so powerful! As we grow and learn, our minds are filled with all kinds of information. Keeping our minds set on God and his ways is something we want to do every day. And starting our day with God is a great way to do just that!

Underline FIX OUR THOUGHTS in the scripture on the last page, then take six different colors and underline each word the verse says to fix your thoughts on in a different color! And the best way to "fix our thoughts" on those things is to know God more through his word. He is all those things! When we spend time with God, his voice becomes louder than the voices in the world.

Here are some practical ways to do this: When we're talking with a friend, we must ask ourselves, "Is this conversation true, or am I sharing something untrue?" When we argue with our parents, we must ask, "Is this lovely and right?"

When we have fixed our thoughts on God and his word, we know better how to be like Christ throughout the day. We go from acting the same way the world does to acting how God wants us to be in the world. And that's like his son, Jesus. Jesus was and is true, honorable, right, pure, lovely, and admirable!

Let's pray together!

Dear God, I want to fix my thoughts on you! Help me to remember the things I read in my Bible every day so I can be more like you. I want to think about things that are true, honorable, right, pure, lovely, and admirable. Help me to praise you all day long!

In Jesus's name, amen.

GO

The world is full of all the things opposite of Philippians 4:8. Can you match the opposites?

Draw a line matching each word on the left with its opposite.

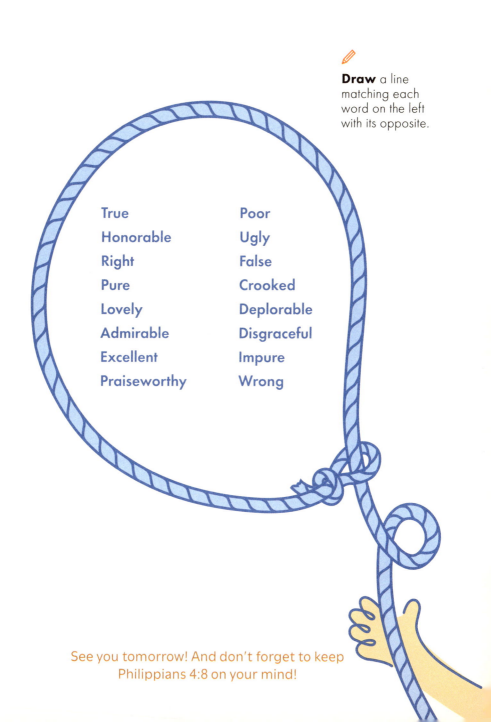

True	Poor
Honorable	Ugly
Right	False
Pure	Crooked
Lovely	Deplorable
Admirable	Disgraceful
Excellent	Impure
Praiseworthy	Wrong

See you tomorrow! And don't forget to keep Philippians 4:8 on your mind!

Day 10: Enjoying God

> **This means that anyone who belongs to Christ has become a new person. The old life is gone; a new life has begun!**
>
> —2 Corinthians 5:17 (NLT)

SCRIPTURE

God is in all we do. God is life! And we don't want to just enjoy God while we spend time with him in Bible study and worship; we want to enjoy him all day long, because he is part of our lives. He is our life! That's what our scripture for today means when it says that "a new life has begun." Our old life is gone, and we have a new life in Christ!

Does that mean you look different on the outside? No. Is your brown hair going to turn blond? No! A new life in Christ isn't a physical change—it's a heart change. When you accept Jesus as your Savior, you begin to live a brand-new life. Before, your sin caused you to live for yourself. Now, you are forgiven for your sin and can live to please and enjoy God in all you do.

> You will show me the way of life, granting me the joy of your presence and the pleasures of living with you forever. —PSALM 16:11 (NLT)

There is joy in the presence of God! Think about that for a minute. The King of Creation, the King of the World, is with us all the time and wants to spend time with us. To enjoy means to take delight or find happiness in something or someone. Do you delight in spending time with God? Do you find happiness when you think about him or talk to him throughout the day? The more you do it, the more you will!

Knowing God is with us and working in our lives brings us such delight and pleasure. He's made us new!

Let's pray together!

Dear God, thank you for a new life in Christ. Help me to be aware of you during the day when I get busy. I want to enjoy your presence in my life no matter what I'm doing. You never leave me! I don't want to leave you. I'm thankful for your love.

In Jesus's name, amen.

GO

You can enjoy God's presence in so many ways because he's in everything you do. He not only gave you his presence to enjoy but he gave you this world too. God's presence is everywhere!

🖉 **Draw** pictures of the God-given things you enjoy. Remember, when you enjoy these things, you are enjoying God's presence because he is with us and in all we do. Examples: *I enjoy God in nature. I enjoy God in music. I enjoy God in food. I enjoy God in people.*

Don't forget to delight in God today! He loves you so much!

Day 11: Our Unchanging God

SCRIPTURE

Jesus Christ is the same yesterday, today, and forever.

—Hebrews 13:8 (ICB)

Our lives are full of change. Even the weather is proof of this—a new season showing up every three months! My favorite season is fall. What is your favorite season? ....

We can count on the seasons to change every year. Fall turns to winter. Winter turns to spring. Spring turns to summer. Summer turns to fall. And then it all begins again!

> The grass dies, and the flowers fall. But the word of our God will live forever — ISAIAH 40:8 (ICB)

The same God who created this amazing world we live in, who created Adam and Eve, who told Noah to build an ark because it was going to rain (even though it had never rained before) is the same God who created you and wants to spend time with you every day.

And God doesn't change! His word never changes. His story never changes. The fact that he doesn't change is very important, because everything you have read about God in the Bible is true and never, ever changes.

You are reading the same stories in the Bible that your parents and grandparents read when they were young. That's fun!

You, on the other hand, change a lot. You grow up. You change your clothes. You change your mind. You might even change your hair color one day!

What else changes in your life?

....

....

Isn't it wonderful that even though you change all the time, and everything in the world seems to be changing, our God never changes? That's good news, because when life feels crazy, we can trust that God still loves us and is in control.

Let's pray together!

Dear God, thank you for always being the same. When everything else around me is changing, including me, you are the same today, yesterday, and forever. That gives me so much peace.

In Jesus's name, amen.

GO

Go outside and grab a rock! Look at it. It won't change if you heat it up, submerge it in water, or drop it (well, at least if you don't drop it really hard). Your rock is pretty durable and unchanging.

✏️ Just like the rock, God doesn't ever change. **Write** Psalm 18:2 on your rock with a marker or paint, and be reminded that God doesn't change.

"The Lord is my rock, my protection, my Savior. My God is my rock." —Psalm 18:2 (ICB)

What a great truth we learned today! See you tomorrow.

Day 12: Our Good Father

SCRIPTURE

The Father has loved us so much! He loved us so much that we are called children of God. And we really are his children. But the people in the world do not understand that we are God's children, because they have not known him.

—1 John 3:1 (ICB)

What does this scripture say about God?

The Father ⬚

He loved us so much we are called ⬚

We really are ⬚

God is our good Father. God is faithful. God knows us. God is love. These are all true characteristics of God, and we know this because the Bible tells us so!

Pull out your Bible and look up these verses:
- 1 John 3:1: He is our Father and he loves us!
- 1 Corinthians 1:9: He is faithful!
- Psalm 139:13–16: He knows us!
- 1 John 4:8: God is love!

A good father's love is unconditional. What does this mean? It means no matter what we do, we are loved. It's hard to imagine a love like that. But God is a good Father, and he loves us no matter what. Even when we make bad decisions, he still loves us and helps us to turn back in the right direction.

He also lavishes us with good gifts. What kind of good gifts? All the kinds of things this world can't offer us, like joy, peace, and comfort.

And because of his big love for us, God has good plans for us. God says, *"I have good plans for you. I don't plan to hurt you. I plan to give you hope and a good future"* JEREMIAH 29:11B (ICB).

A very popular verse, John 3:16 (ICB), says, *"For God loved the world so much that he gave his only Son. God gave his Son so that whoever believes in him may not be lost, but have eternal life."*

According to John 3:16, how did God show his love for the world?

He's such a good Father that he made a way to spend forever with him!

Let's pray together!

Dear God, you are a good Father to me. You loved me so much that you sent your son Jesus to this earth to live and die for me. I'll never be able to thank you enough for showing me that kind of love. Help me to love others like you love them.

In Jesus's name, amen.

GO

God is a good Father to us every day! He loves us when we don't deserve it. He gave us family and friends. And he protects us from storms.

 Draw a picture that shows how God has been a good Father to you this week!

God is with you today! Keep smiling, and we'll see you tomorrow!

Day 13: Growing Good Fruit

SCRIPTURE

But the fruit of the Spirit is love, joy, peace, patience, kindness, goodness, faithfulness, gentleness, self-control; against such things there is no law.

—Galatians 5:22–23 (ESV)

Congratulations! You have been having consistent time with God. Are you starting to get into a rhythm? Are you finding it easier to make time to spend with him?

What is one thing you have learned about yourself or God so far?

Remember back in Day 5 when we talked about the need to stick close to God like a branch stays attached to a tree? Today, let's talk about all the good fruit you can produce by sticking close to God!

Our time with God every day has a purpose. It is to produce fruit in our life. We are born with sin in our lives, stuff that tries to separate us from God. That's why we need Jesus and the Bible. By reading God's word every day, we stick close to God and learn how to live a life that makes God and us happy.

Now, I know you are a person, but for right now, pretend you are a tree growing fruit. Stick your arms and legs out wide like branches!

You don't want to be growing sour, old, brown fruit, do you? No! You want to grow beautiful, yummy, useful fruit that represents all things good. The Bible calls these the fruits of the spirit—things that make us more like God. In the scripture above, underline all the fruits of the spirit.

When we choose to say no to sin, we are replacing bad fruit (hate, impatience, and meanness) with good fruit (love, patience, and kindness). And the time we spend with God helps us grow these fruits!

Are you a loving person? How do you treat others? That's a serious question for a young person, isn't it? Think about it for a minute.

As you get to know God more and start to grow godly fruit in your life, everyone around you will see it and know that God is at the center of your life.

Let's pray together!

Dear God, I'm so thankful for my time with you! Every day we spend together, I am learning so much about what it means to follow you. As I grow closer to you, help my life to grow your fruit. I want to grow love, joy, peace, patience, kindness, goodness, faithfulness, gentleness, and self-control!

In Jesus's name, amen.

GO

Find all the fruits of the spirit in the word search below!

```
H G I Y O J I R T E L V I H F
H E P A T I E N C E J O Y Z A
A N F J H F B A D Z X N O I I
A T G R D S V J V W G N J P T
Y L R N B H G S V R D K L G H
M E P E A C E D K I I G R A F
Y N S E L F C O N T R O L L U
D E A W G N V R I Z I O Y G L
B S Q O C V H B V C M D Q U N
N S V Y K P A L Q Q U N H J E
U M E W D C K I N D N E S S S
L Z S T E F C V A C C S Q B S
K V T D J J O Q V A X S L R X
V O J J B E W Z E A H L U L N
W G L O V E M G N N P F G W J
```

Love
Joy
Peace
Patience
Kindness
Goodness
Faithfulness
Gentleness
Self-control

✏️ Did you find all the words? Now take time to **write** down what you think each of those words mean!

Love:	Kindness:
Joy:	Goodness:
Peace:	Faithfulness:
Patience:	Gentleness:
	Self-control:

Spending time with God is fun, isn't it? See you tomorrow!

Day 14: Making the Most of Our Time

SCRIPTURE

So be very careful how you live. Do not live like those who are not wise. Live wisely. I mean that you should use every chance you have for doing good, because these are evil times.

—Ephesians 5:15–16 (ICB)

How we live our lives is important. We don't want to live like foolish people who don't care how they live. When God is the center of our lives, we care about how we act and how our actions affect others.

We want to represent Jesus in all that we do. Wherever we go, we take him with us. So, we want to be careful how we act and talk.

Pretend you put on this name tag every day! Would you act differently if you put this name tag on?

Read the verse of the day one more time. How are we called to live?

What does living wisely mean to you? Share some things you can do today that show you are living wisely. Example: *Obey my parents.*

How do we know how to live wisely?

Let's see what the Bible has to say:

> But the wisdom that comes from God is like this: First, it is pure. Then it is also peaceful, gentle, and easy to please. This wisdom is always ready to help those who are troubled and to do good for others. This wisdom is always fair and honest. —JAMES 3:17 (ICB)

You got it! Wisdom comes from God! You are learning to live wisely by spending time with God every day. You have hit the wisdom jackpot!

Let's pray together!

Dear God, I'm so thankful for my time with you! Every day we spend together, I am learning so much about what it means to follow you. Please help me to be wise and to do good to everyone around me. I want to be more like you every day.

In Jesus's name, amen.

GO

Living wisely can be hard some days. It means we have to *think first* and then ask, "What is the wise thing to do? What is right? What is wrong?"

Circle all the answers below that show wisdom. *(Hint: You can circle more than one!)*

When your friend needs help finding something they lost, what is wise to do?

- Help her find it
- Walk away and not help
- Ask an adult to help

When one of your parents asks you a question, the wise thing to do is to . . .

- Lie
- Tell them the truth
- Ignore them

If you see some money on the ground, what is wise to do?

- Ask around if someone lost it
- Walk away
- Keep it for yourself

When a new student in class or church sits by themselves at lunch, the wise thing to do is to . . .

- Keep sitting with my friends
- Sit with the new kid
- Invite them to sit with me and my friends

What other wise decisions have you or your friends made this week?

Think before you act today! That's the wise thing to do.
See you tomorrow!

Day 15: The Holy Spirit in Us

SCRIPTURE

Don't you realize that your body is the temple of the Holy Spirit, who lives in you and was given to you by God? You do not belong to yourself, for God bought you with a high price. So you must honor God with your body.

—1 Corinthians 6:19–20 (NLT)

Congratulations! You have completed three weeks of devotional time with God. When we read the Bible, pray, and worship, we feel closer to him. You've been doing that for fifteen days!

Yesterday, we talked about living our lives wisely, so today we're going to talk about how God plans to help us do just that.

It's easy to think that God is just at church. Or just with us when we pray. But he is always with us because of what his son, Jesus, did on the cross. Jesus died for our sins on the cross, rose from the grave, and defeated death! Afterward, in John 15:26, Jesus told his disciples that God would send a helper to help them accomplish all God called them to.

Do you know who that helper is?

That helper is God's Holy Spirit! When we put our trust in Jesus, God's Spirit comes to live in us. That way, God is always with us!

Read today's scripture one more time and answer these questions:

Who gave the Holy Spirit to you?

What does today's scripture say we should do because the Holy Spirit is in us?

So, everywhere we go, we have God with us and we *represent God*! The way we treat our bodies (the house of the Holy Spirit), and the way we treat those around us, shows people that God is living inside of us. That's a big responsibility, isn't it?

Well, the good news is that you have the Holy Spirit to help you!

Let's pray together!

Thank you, God, for giving your son, Jesus, for me! And thank you that you have also given me your Holy Spirit. Help me to remember that I represent you wherever I go!

In Jesus's name, amen.

GO

Do you have a balloon or beach ball in your home? Before you inflate it, there isn't much of a use for it and it's not very fun when it's flat, is it? But if you blow air from your lungs into the balloon or ball, it suddenly becomes what it was made for! You are created the same way. When God's Holy Spirit comes to live inside you, your true self comes to life. You are filled with God's Spirit and you can live with purpose.

If you have time, **blow up a balloon** or beach ball. Show a family member or friend how you are different because the Holy Spirit lives in you.

What are some ways you will live differently because of the Spirit in you?

Don't forget, you represent Christ wherever you go. See you tomorrow!

Day 16: God Is Our Friend

SCRIPTURE

The greatest love a person can show is to die for his friends. You are my friends if you do what I command you.

—John 15:13–14 (ICB)

Friendship is a gift from God! Do you have a good friend? Maybe you have more than one good friend! Write the name(s) of your friend(s) below (and remember your siblings or parents can be friends too)!

My Friends:

....

....

Now, let's thank God for those friends really quickly! Pray with me.

Thank you, God, for my friends. They are a blessing from you, and I am very thankful. I pray [name your friends] know how much you love them. Let me be a true friend to them like you are to me!

Have you ever had a friend move away because their parents got a job out of town or maybe they needed to move to be close to other family members? Have you ever had to move away from a friend, and it made you sad? It's hard to leave friends.

But friendship with God is different from any earthly friendships we have. When we accept Jesus as our savior, friendship with him is forever!

Did you know that Jesus had a group of friends who walked with him throughout his ministry on earth? They loved him, listened to him, and followed his commands. They modeled for us what walking with God looks like. They were called disciples.

When you feel like you don't have a friend (we all feel that way sometimes), remember that God is your forever friend. He hears you, sees you, and knows you. He'll never move away from you. If you don't feel like he is close, then open your Bible, pray, and worship. Then you'll feel his closeness again.

Let's pray together!

Thank you for friendship, God. You are my forever friend.
I pray that I will love my friends well, just like you love me. Help me to love you, listen to you, and follow your commands all my life.

In Jesus's name, amen.

Friendship is a gift from God. Take time today to write to a friend (on a notecard or paper) and let them know how special they are to you! Maybe even include today's scripture!

On a seperate piece of paper, **draw** a picture of the two of you having fun! Take it to them, or mail it if they aren't close by. Pray for them before you send it!

My friend's name:

Isn't spending time with God so much fun? See you tomorrow!

Day 17: Hearing God's Voice

SCRIPTURE

My sheep listen to my voice.
I know them, and they follow me.

—John 10:27 (ICB)

All through the Bible we read about sheep and shepherds. When Jesus was born in Bethlehem, who were the first to visit him? *(Hint: If you don't know, look up Luke 2:15–20 in your Bible.)*

That's right, it was the shepherds! Do you know what shepherds do? They protect and herd sheep. That means they keep the sheep together and moving in the right direction. The shepherds are like the sheep's father.

The Bible often calls Jesus the Good Shepherd. In the scripture for today, Jesus was teaching in the temple and answering questions about who he is. He revealed that his sheep are the only ones who will know who he really is. His response was, "My sheep listen to my voice. I know them, and they follow me."

Jesus is the Good Shepherd, and his children are the sheep. We will hear his voice more clearly as we get to know him better. And, like we learned on Day 15, God's Holy Spirit will come and live in us when we invite him.

We don't have to wait to go to church to hear God. We can hear him throughout the day, in our time with God, playing sports, or eating a meal. God is in us. He's talking to us all the time through his word, the beauty around us, and even through our friends and family. We just need to listen!

Have you ever been lost? If you have, the best feeling in the world is hearing the voice of your parents calling your name! You recognize their voice immediately because you are listening for them. When we spend time with God every day, we are closer to him and can hear him more clearly throughout the day.

Let's pray together!

You are my Good Shepherd! Help me to be a sheep that listens to your word and shares it with my friends and family. When I'm wandering, lost, or not listening, bring me back to you. I always want to hear your voice.

In Jesus's name, amen.

GO

Fill in the scripture for today!

"My _____ listen to my voice. I know them, and they _____ me." _____ 10:27

There are six sheep pictures below. The first sheep has no differences, but the others have a small difference each. Can you spot the differences?

Circle the difference on each sheep.

Great job today. See you tomorrow!

Day 18: Knowing God's Truth

SCRIPTURE

**And you will know the truth,
and the truth will set you free.**

—John 8:32 (NLT)

What is the opposite of the word *true?* ....
(Hint: Keep reading for the answer.)

In our scripture for today, Jesus was showing his followers (and us) that what he teaches is true and that this truth will set his people free, if they believe!

Jesus is the truth. And through Scripture and the Holy Spirit, we can know the truth. Spending time with God every day helps guide us. As we know, our sins keep us from God, but when we are guided by his truth, we can make good decisions that please him. Jesus died for us so we could be set free from sin and be close to God again.

The truth sets us free!

Check out John 14:6 in your Bible:

> Jesus answered, "I am the way. And I am the truth and the life. The only way to the Father is through me" (ICB).

Jesus is making sure his followers know that he is the true and only way to God. There are false teachers in the world—people who tell us there are other ways to have a relationship with God. But the Bible reminds us that accepting Jesus is the only way to spend forever with God. Anything else is *false!*

You can remember it this way: Jesus is the *truth*, and he sets us *free!* (Oh yeah! Did you figure out the answer from above? It's FALSE!)

Let's pray together!

Dear God, just like we talked about yesterday, I want to hear you and I want to know the truth. Protect me from false teachers who aren't speaking the truth. Thank you for your word and Holy Spirit that help me know the truth.

In Jesus's name, amen.

GO

Time to put your knowledge to the test!

✏️ **Answer** the questions below with True (T) or False (F).

☐ Jesus is God's son.

☐ The Bible is true.

☐ *My Time with God Devotional* will make me a better soccer player.

☐ *My Time with God Devotional* will help me to know God.

☐ God's telephone number is Jeremiah 12:3. *(Hint: Day 3 will have a clue!)*

☐ God loves me, sees me, hears me, and talks to me.

☐ Believing in Jesus is the only way to God.

☐ God changes all the time.

☐ When I worship God, he is pleased.

☐ Prayer is talking and listening to God.

(Answers: T, T, F, T, F, T, T, F, T, T)

You did awesome, way to go! See you tomorrow.

Day 19: God's Loving Discipline

SCRIPTURE

"I am the true vine; my Father is the gardener. He cuts off every branch of mine that does not produce fruit. And he trims and cleans every branch that produces fruit so that it will produce even more fruit."

—John 15:1–2 (ICB)

Have you ever made a bad choice and your parents had to discipline you? Of course you have—we all have! Most parents don't love to discipline their kids because it hurts their hearts. But parents know that discipline is good for us, to help us learn a lesson, even though no one enjoys it!

God is the same way. He loves us so much that sometimes he must discipline us when we are going the wrong way. And sometimes, even though we didn't do anything wrong, hard things still happen to us. It happened to Jesus too.

That's what Jesus is explaining to his followers in our scripture for today. Answer the following questions about the verse above.

Who does Jesus say he is?

Who does Jesus say God is?

What does God do to the branches that don't produce fruit?

What about the ones that do produce fruit?

Jesus is the vine. (We talked about this on Day 5.) And God is the gardener! In the scripture, it says that God "cuts off" the branches that don't produce fruit and "trims and cleans" every one that does produce good fruit.

When God disciplines us ("cuts off" the bad branches), we know it's because he loves us so much. He wants us to grow closer to him through discipline. And on the plain old hard days, where we didn't make a wrong choice but still suffered, God uses those moments to "clean and trim" our fruit. Again, to make us more like him! God's discipline always comes with his love. They go together.

Let's pray together!

Dear God, it's hard to be disciplined. Help me to know you love me even when you must discipline me. Thank you for loving me so much that you don't just let me do what I want to do all the time. Thank you for caring about all of me and helping me to be more like you.

In Jesus's name, amen.

GO

God is the gardener. Jesus is the vine. We are the branches.

Color the lemon tree to help illustrate this truth from God's word. When you are in your yard or out for a walk, remember our scripture for today. Let's be branches that grow good fruit!

Way to go! It's hard to believe tomorrow is our last day together. See you then!

Day 20: Becoming like Jesus

> **SCRIPTURE**
>
> This is what the Lord says: "Wise men must not brag about their wisdom. Strong men must not brag about their strength. Rich men must not brag about their money. But if someone wants to brag, let him brag about this: Let him brag that he understands and knows me. Let him brag that I am the Lord. Let him brag that I am kind and fair. Let him brag that I do things that are right on earth. This kind of bragging pleases me," says the Lord.
>
> —Jeremiah 9:23-24 (ICB)

God tells us not to brag about anything we are able to do or anything that we have. In the verse above, take a red marker and underline everything that God tells us *not* to brag about.

Why shouldn't we brag about our wisdom, strength, or money? Because everything we have comes from God. So, if we're going to brag, then we should brag on God! In the verses for today, take a green marker and underline everything that God tells us to brag about.

In this life, knowing and understanding God is the best thing we can do! And the more we get to know God, the more we become like his son, Jesus. Becoming like Jesus is the goal every day. Through this daily devotional, you've been learning how to study God's word, pray, and spend time with God.

Look up Psalm 46:10 in your Bible.

> "Be still and know that I am God!"

That is the reason we meet with God every day and why this devotional was written for you! When we become still and meet with God, we get to know him better and our lives begin to change.

But remember, the older you get, the busier you will get. Making it a priority *now* to spend time with God every day is something you will be happy you did for the rest of your life.

Let's pray together!

Dear God, thank you for your word, which teaches me so much about you! I want to continue to learn and grow in my relationship with you. I pray I look more like Jesus every day. Help me to live like you so that my family and community know you more too! I love you, God.

In Jesus's name, amen.

GO

Why is God's word so special to you? Show this picture to someone in your family and ask them to pray for you as you continue to grow to be more like Jesus.

 Draw a picture of you studying God's word below.

You did it! You spent twenty days with God! Keep going, there is so much to learn about God and his word.

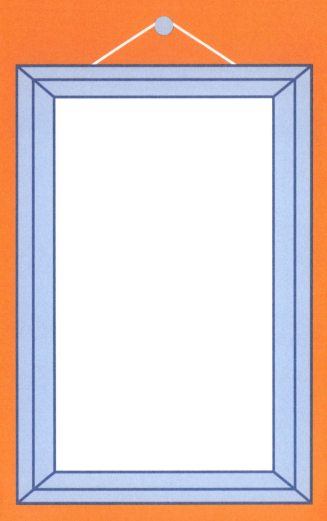

Draw a picture of yourself with your completed journal.

"Be still, and know that I am God."

—Psalm 46:10

About First15

Spending consistent time alone with God can be a struggle. We're busier—and more stressed—than ever. But still, we know it's important to spend unhindered time with our Creator. We know we need to read his word, pray, and worship him.

First 15 bridges the gap between desire and reality, helping you establish the rhythm of meaningful, daily experiences in God's presence. First 15 answers the critical questions:

- Why should I spend time alone with God?
- How do I spend time alone with God?
- How do I get the most out of my time alone with God?
- How can I become more consistent in my time alone with God?

And by answering these questions through daily devotionals, we help people practice the rhythm of meeting with God while experiencing the incredible gift of his loving presence.

To learn more about First 15, download our app or visit our website: *First15.org*. The First 15 devotional is also available via email and podcast.